Blastoff! Readers are carefully developed by literacy experts to build reading stamina and move students toward fluency by combining standards-based content with developmentally appropriate text.

 Level 1 provides the most support through repetition of high-frequency words, light text, predictable sentence patterns, and strong visual support.

 Level 2 offers early readers a bit more challenge through varied sentences, increased text load, and text-supportive special features.

 Level 3 advances early-fluent readers toward fluency through increased text load, less reliance on photos, advancing concepts, longer sentences, and more complex special features.

★ **Blastoff! Universe**

This edition first published in 2026 by Bellwether Media, Inc.

No part of this publication may be reproduced in whole or in part without written permission of the publisher. For information regarding permission, write to Bellwether Media, Inc., Attention: Permissions Department, 3500 American Blvd W, Suite 150, Bloomington, MN 55431.

Library of Congress Cataloging-in-Publication Data

LC record for Mandarin available at: https://lccn.loc.gov/2025019038

Text copyright © 2026 by Bellwether Media, Inc. BLASTOFF! READERS and associated logos are trademarks and/or registered trademarks of Bellwether Media, Inc. Bellwether Media is a division of FlutterBee Education Group.

Editor: Suzane Nguyen   Designer: Andrea Schneider

Printed in the United States of America, North Mankato, MN.

bēi zǐ

Table of Contents

Nǐ Hǎo!	4
At Home	8
At School	12
After School	16
Wǎn Ān!	20
Glossary	22
To Learn More	23
Index	24

Nǐ hǎo! Let's learn Mandarin Chinese or *Zhōng wén*. It is a **tonal language**.

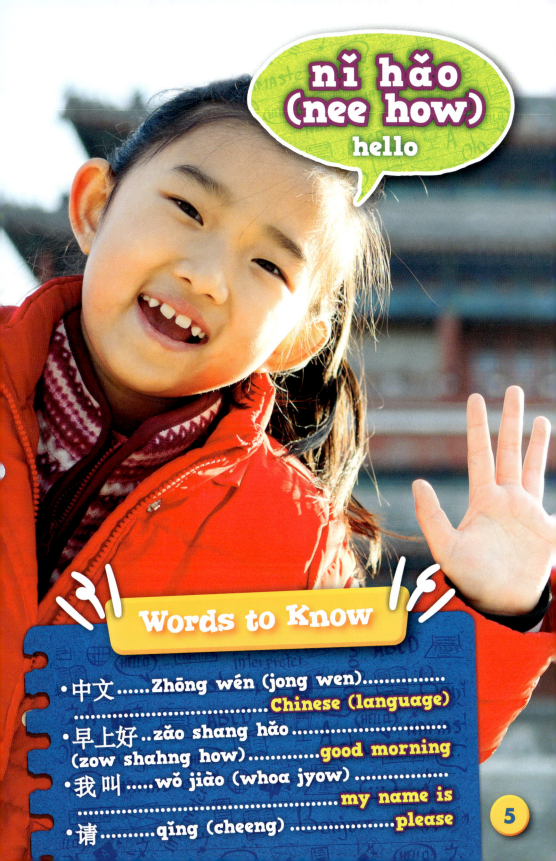

nǐ hǎo (nee how)
hello

Words to Know

- 中文 ...... Zhōng wén (jong wen) .... Chinese (language)
- 早上好 .. zǎo shang hǎo .... (zow shahng how) .... good morning
- 我叫 ..... wǒ jiǎo (whoa jyow) .... my name is
- 请 .... qǐng (cheeng) .... please

Mandarin is spoken in China, Taiwan, and Singapore. It uses **characters**.

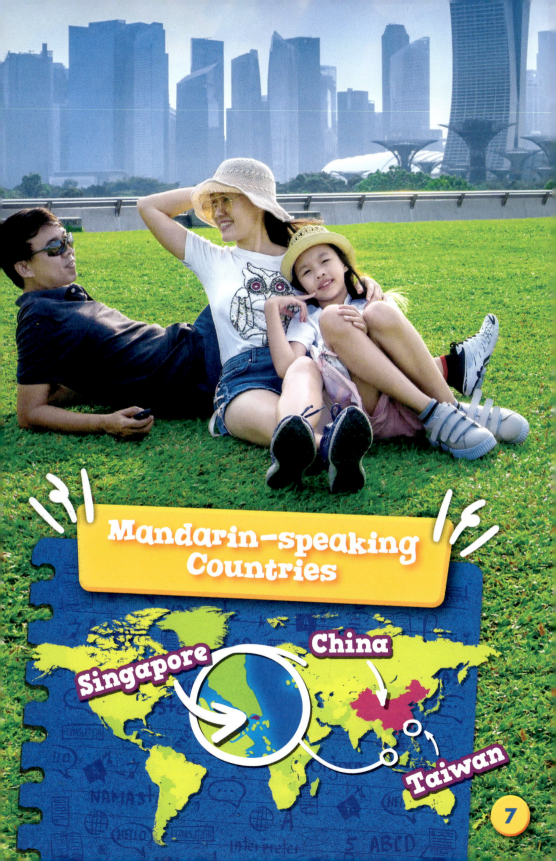

At Home

Min lives in a *fáng zi*. She eats with her *bà ba* and *mā ma*.

gǒu

Words to Know

- 爸爸 .. bà ba (bah bah) .... **dad**
- 妈妈 .. mā ma (mah mah) .... **mom**
- 爷爷 .. yé ye (yea yea) .... **grandpa (father's father)**
- 奶奶 .. nǎi nai (ny ny) .... **grandma (father's mother)**
- 狗 ...... gǒu (goh) .... **dog**
- 房子 .. fáng zi (fong zeh) .... **house**

bēi zǐ

Words to Know

- 早饭 .. zǎo fàn (zow fahn) ...... breakfast
- 碗 ...... wǎn (wahn) .... bowl
- 杯子 .. bēi zǐ (bay-zuh) .... cup
- 桌子 .. zhuō zǐ (jo-zuh) .... table

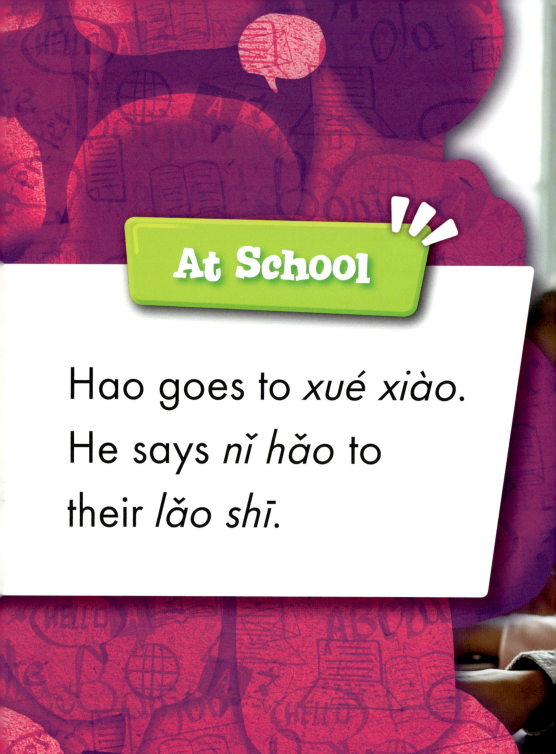

At School

Hao goes to *xué xiào*.
He says *nǐ hǎo* to
their *lǎo shī*.

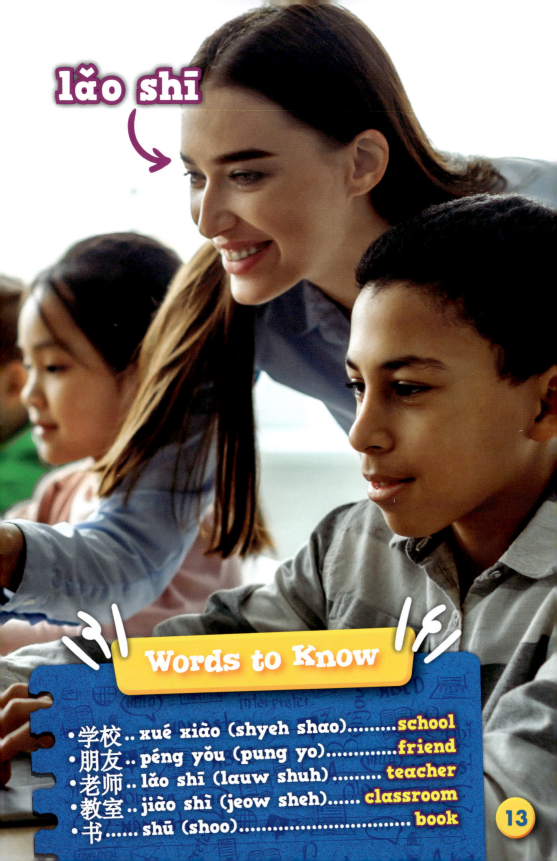

lǎo shī

Words to Know

- 学校 .. xué xiào (shyeh shao) .... school
- 朋友 .. péng yǒu (pung yo) .... friend
- 老师 .. lǎo shī (lauw shuh) .... teacher
- 教室 .. jiào shì (jeow sheh) ...... classroom
- 书 ...... shū (shoo) .... book

13

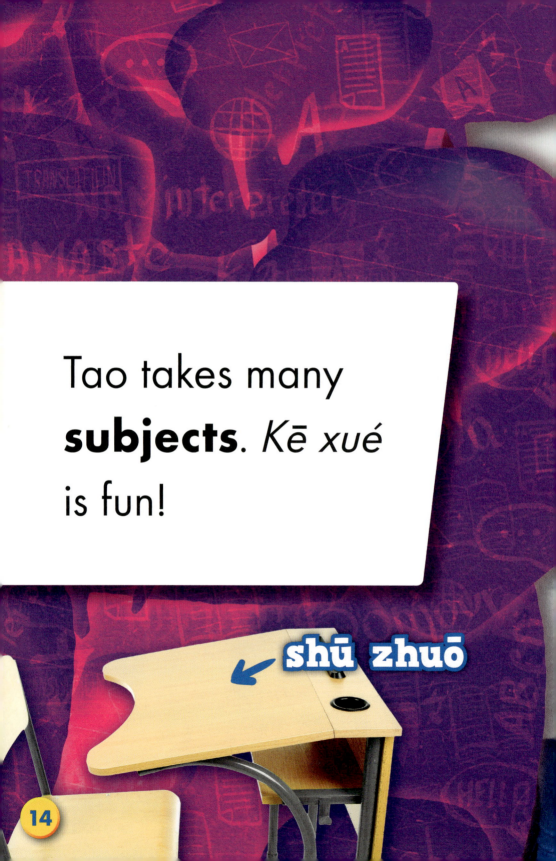

Tao takes many **subjects**. *Kē xué* is fun!

shū zhuō

Count in Mandarin

一 .... yī ...... (ee) 1
二 .... ér ...... (are) 2
三 .... sān .... (san) 3
四 .... sì ...... (suh) 4
五 .... wǔ ..... (woo) .. 5
六 .... liù ..... (lio) 6
七 .... qī .... (chi) 7
八 .... bā ...... (ba) 8
九 .... jiǔ ..... (geo) ... 9
十 .... shí ..... (shuh) 10

kē xué

Words to Know

- 科学 .. kē xué (kuh shyeh) .... **science**
- 书桌 .. shū zhuō (shoo joh) .... **desk**
- 铅笔 .. qiān bǐ (chee-yan bee) .... **pencil**
- 纸 ...... zhǐ (jeh) .... **paper**

After School

After school, Bao practices *yīng yǔ*. He plays *lán qiú*, too.

qiú

Words to Know

- 英语 .. yīng yǔ (ying yoo) .... English
- 导师 .. dǎo shī (dow shee) .... tutor
- 篮球 .. lán qiú (lahn chyo) ..... basketball
- 球 .... qiú (chyo) .... ball
- 运动 .. yùn dòng (yoon dong) .... sports

Chen eats *wǎn fàn* with his family. They eat with **chopsticks**.

Words to Know

- 晚饭 .. wǎn fàn (wahn fan) .... **dinner**
- 米飯 .. mǐ fàn (mee-fahn) .... **rice**
- 蔬菜 .. shū cài (shoo tsai) ...... **vegetables**
- 豆腐 .. dòu fu (doe foo) .... **tofu**
- 茶 ...... chá (chah) .... **tea**

mǐ fàn

19

Wǎn Ān!

Yue does *zuò yè* before bed. *Xiè xiè* for today! *Wǎn ān*!

Words to Know

- 作业 .. zuò yè (zo yea) .... homework
- 请 .... qǐng (ching) .... please
- 谢谢 .. xiè xiè (shyeh shyeh) ... thank you
- 床 ...... chuáng (chwahng) .... bed
- 再见 .. zài jiàn (z-eye j-yin) ..... good bye

**wǎn ān
(wahn ahn)**
good night

Glossary

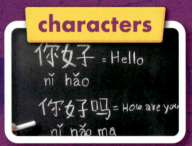

characters

written symbols used to write Chinese

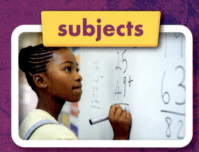

subjects

areas of study in school, like math or science

chopsticks

pairs of wooden sticks used to pick up and eat food

tonal language

a language where the sounds in words can change their meanings

congee

a soupy dish made from rice

To Learn More

AT THE LIBRARY

Davies, Monika. *China*. Minneapolis, Minn.: Bellwether Media, 2023.

Davis, Bela. *Intro to Chinese*. Minneapolis, Minn.: Abdo Kids, 2024.

Wong, Fanny. *See and Say Mandarin*. North Mankato, Minn.: Capstone, 2025.

ON THE WEB

FACTSURFER

Factsurfer.com gives you a safe, fun way to find more information.

1. Go to www.factsurfer.com.

2. Enter "Mandarin" into the search box and click 🔍.

3. Select your book cover to see a list of related content.

Index

bed, 20
characters, 6
China, 6
chopsticks, 18
congee, 10
count in Mandarin, 15
eats, 8, 18
family, 8, 18
food, 10, 18
good night, 21
hello, 5
home, 8
map, 7
plays, 16
practices, 16

school, 12, 14, 16
Singapore, 6
subjects, 14
Taiwan, 6
tonal language, 4
words to know, 5, 9, 11, 13, 15, 17, 19, 21

The images in this book are reproduced through the courtesy of: wee design, front cover; siriratsavett88, p. 3; kool99, pp. 4-5; oneSHUTTER oneMEMORY, pp. 6-7; Dmytro Titov, p. 8 (gǒu); Marcus Chung, pp. 8-9; Tunagaga, p. 10 (congee); ucchie79, pp. 10-11; Prostock-studio, pp. 12-13; Africa Studio, p. 14 (shū zhuō); Monkey Business Images, pp. 14-15; GAYSORN, pp. 16-17; Nitr, p. 18 (shū cài); Blue Jean Images, pp. 18-19; miniseries/ Getty Images, pp. 20-21; toa555, p. 22 (characters); Sammyvision/ Getty Images, p. 22 (chopsticks); GoodRNG, p. 22 (congee); Rido, p. 22 (subjects); Pixel-Shot, p. 22 (tonal language).